# WORLD WAR I SPY STORIES

BY MARTHA LONDON

MOMENTUM

Published by The Child's World®
1980 Lookout Drive • Mankato, MN 56003-1705
800-599-READ • www.childsworld.com

Photographs ©: Everett Historical/Shutterstock
Images, cover (left), 1 (left) 5, 9, 15, 20, 21; Chepko
Danil Vitalevich/Shutterstock Images, cover (right),
1 (right); The History Collection/Alamy, 6; Red Line
Editorial, 8; Chronicle/Alamy, 11; AP Images, 12, 17,
18, 24; Trinity Mirror/Mirrorpix/Alamy, 22; Illustrated
London News Ltd/Pantheon/SuperStock, 26;
Peter Moulton/Shutterstock Images, 27

ISBN 9781503844810 (Reinforced Library Binding)
ISBN 9781503847309 (Portable Document Format)
ISBN 9781503848498 (Online Multi-user eBook)
LCCN 2019956595

Printed in the United States of America

# CONTENTS

MOMENTUM

# FAST FACTS

## World War I History

▶ In total, 30 countries fought in World War I (1914–1918). The Allied powers included Great Britain, France, Belgium, Russia, and the United States. The Central powers included Germany and Austria-Hungary. The war was caused in part by rising tensions in Europe.

▶ On November 11, 1918, Germany was the last country to agree to end the war.

## Spies and Secret Messages

▶ Spies carried information across borders. Dogs and pigeons also carried messages.

▶ Both sides used telephones to spy and spread information. German forces found a way to listen in on Allied phone calls. They were also very good at breaking Allied communication codes. To fix this, Allied forces teamed up with Native American soldiers from the Choctaw, Comanche, and Cheyenne Nations, among others. Native Americans used their languages to relay messages because the Germans could not understand them.

▲ **German soldiers often used machine guns in World War I.**

▶ German agents used coded bread loaves. Day-old loaves had a number stamped on them. They were put in a bakery window. The number matched an agent's number. This helped German agents know when they needed to contact other German officials.

▶ Allied and Central powers used aerial photographs. The photographs showed the movements of enemy armies.

# CHAPTER ONE

# LOUISE DE BETTIGNIES

The moon was a tiny sliver in the sky. Louise de Bettignies wove between trees in the dark forest. She needed to cross into the Netherlands from Belgium. A loud blast filled the air as a mine exploded in the distance. De Bettignies felt her heart pump faster, and she reminded herself to be careful. German soldiers had buried mines throughout the forest.

De Bettignies had a job to do. A coded letter detailing German movements was tucked in the back of her boot. Her skirt was muddy from the long walk through the countryside in the rain. De Bettignies adjusted the oiled jacket that she was wearing in case the rain started again. De Bettignies was a spy, and her codename was Alice Dubois. She was the head of a spy group called the Alice Network.

◄ Louise de Bettignies was born
in France. In addition to French,
de Bettignies spoke German and English.

De Bettignies made several journeys between Belgium and the Netherlands. The border between Belgium and the Netherlands was heavily guarded by German soldiers. That made it difficult for Allied soldiers to get information from Belgium. But de Bettignies took the risk. Once she got to the Netherlands, she could safely hand messages to British agents.

## EUROPEAN COUNTRIES INVOLVED IN WORLD WAR I

- Central powers
- Allied powers
- Neutral

Finland
Sweden
Norway
United Kingdom
Denmark
Netherlands
Russia
Germany
Belgium
Austria-Hungary
France
Romania
Italy
Bulgaria
Serbia
Portugal
Turkey
Spain
Switzerland
Albania
Greece

▲ **The Germans invaded Belgium in August 1914 in order to get to northern France.**

The Netherlands was **neutral** in World War I. The people there would not stop her from passing along her information. The next day, de Bettignies arrived at a **checkpoint** in a Belgian town.

German soldiers walked around carrying guns. An electric fence hummed just outside of town. De Bettignies needed to go through the city gates. She brushed some mud from her skirts. She did not want German soldiers to suspect that she had been hiking in the woods all night.

At the checkpoint, de Bettignies handed her fake identification papers to a German officer who wore a crisp green coat. As he looked at the papers, de Bettignies started talking endlessly about the weather. She shifted the bag she held tightly in her arms. As she talked, she could tell the soldier was getting frustrated. He didn't want to listen to her.

## THE ALICE NETWORK

The Alice Network was a collection of 80 men and women. They spied on the Central powers. The spies had many different jobs. Some worked in churches. Others were doctors. Many of the spies were located in France. German forces took over part of the country. Spies gained information from the German soldiers who were occupying the country.

▲ **A statue of de Bettignies was put up in France to recognize her work.**

Eventually, the soldier pushed her through the checkpoint. De Bettignies let out a pent-up breath. A smile flashed across her face as she stepped into the Netherlands. The message was safe.

# CHAPTER TWO

# FRANZ VON RINTELEN

**F**ranz von Rintelen sat at a desk in an office. He was a German living in the United States. He was loyal to Germany. It was December 1914, and the war had started. The United States was not yet directly involved, but it was selling things such as weapons to Allied forces. Von Rintelen wanted to stop this from happening. He looked at his watch. Walter Scheele, a German chemist, would be arriving any minute.

The office door was suddenly opened, and Scheele walked in. He shook out his coat and hung it on a hook. He sat in a chair across from von Rintelen. Scheele pulled a lead tube out of his coat pocket. It was bigger than a pen. Von Rintelen's eyebrows raised slightly. The object looked useless. What could he possibly do with something so small? But as Scheele explained how the object worked, von Rintelen understood how clever it was.

◀ **Franz von Rintelen pretended to be from Switzerland in order to get into the United States.**

The tube was small enough that no one would notice it. The device was hollow, and inside were two types of **acids**. When the acids mixed, it caused a fire. A disc separated the acids and would dissolve slowly depending on how thick the disc was. It gave von Rintelen the option of planting the device, getting safely away, and knowing that the fire would not start for a while. Then, when the fire eventually burned out, the lead tube completely melted away. There would be no **evidence** that von Rintelen had planted it. Instead, people would think the fires were just accidents.

Von Rintelen paid Scheele for his invention. He was already thinking about who he could **recruit** to help him plant this device.

## PREPARING FOR WORLD WAR I

In 1912, Walter Nicolai was the head of an intelligence group in Germany. The war had not started yet. But tensions were rising in Europe. Nicolai called on his agents. He sent them to Russia and France. Coded **telegrams** and letters detailed whether the countries were preparing for a war. Spies sent information about whether factories were making weapons. They also noted if soldiers were training.

▲ The United States didn't enter the war until Germany kept attacking U.S. ships. In April 1917, President Woodrow Wilson asked Congress to declare war on Germany.

Later, von Rintelen stood before a group of men. They listened carefully as he talked. Von Rintelen wanted to stop U.S. ships from giving supplies, such as **ammunition**, to the Allies.

Von Rintelen planned on using Scheele's device to do this. Small fires would halt shipments. But first, he needed to find a place to build them.

The group left the office for the transport docks. That was where ships with ammunition for the Allies were located. The docks were loud and busy. Workers rushed from point to point. Ships needed repairs, and ammunition and weapons needed to be loaded.

The men in the group stayed focused. They found a ship where they could build the bombs. No one would suspect them.

A few weeks later, a ship with a load of ammunition was bound for England. Von Rintelen had his chance. One of the men took several of Von Rintelen's devices on board and planted it. When the ship left the harbor, the crew had no idea the devices were in the cargo. While the ship was at sea in 1915, fires broke out. The crew had to dump the cargo. If they did not, the ship would have exploded. Von Rintelen's plan worked. That time, valuable supplies never reached the Allies.

In 1916, there was an explosion on Black Tom ▶ Island in New York Harbor. The island had a lot of ammunition. Later, officials would find out that some German agents were responsible.

# CHAPTER THREE

# MARTHE CNOCKAERT

**G**erman soldiers laughed at tables. Dim lights lined the walls of the Belgium café, and Marthe Cnockaert moved from the counter to the waiting customers. She carried drinks and food on a tray. In the back, her father washed dishes. The sound of clinking plates and mugs filled the room.

As Cnockaert set the drinks down, the German soldiers looked up at her. They thanked her and continued on with their conversations. The soldiers liked Cnockaert. She treated many of them at the hospital where she also worked as a nurse.

Cnockaert smiled and walked slowly to another table. She listened for any important information about the German army. Cnockaert was a spy for Belgium. While German soldiers stayed in Cnockaert's town, she gave information to a network of Allied spies.

◄ **Many German soldiers were in Belgium during the war.**

▲ **Soldiers sometimes had to get through barbed wire to reach the opposing army.**

At the end of the evening, Cnockaert left the café. Lamps lit the sidewalk. She had not gotten any useful information, but it was okay. Cnockaert would work at the hospital the next day. The injured German soldiers loved to talk.

▲ **A lot of buildings in Europe were destroyed during the war, including many in France.**

The next morning, Cnockaert walked between the rows of beds. The patients there were young. Cnockaert liked many of the soldiers in the hospital. But she knew she had to help her country.

Cnockaert sat on the edge of a German soldier's bed. He had been in the hospital for a couple of weeks. He was almost ready to be released. After so many days in the same place, the soldier wanted to talk. Cnockaert listened, and she asked questions.

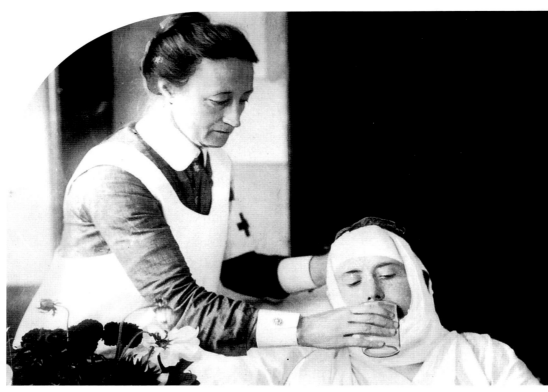

▲ **Nurses played an important role in helping soldiers during the war.**

The soldier worked closely with German commanders. He told Cnockaert about the German army's plans to move a large army troop. Cnockaert's heart raced. But she didn't show her emotions. The soldier could not know how she felt.

On a break, Cnockaert wrote a coded note. She stuck it in her pocket. After her shift, she needed to find Canteen Ma. Canteen Ma was an older woman who sold vegetables and fruit in the town. The Germans thought she was harmless. But Ma was another spy.

Cnockaert finished her shift in the early afternoon. She headed toward the town square. Canteen Ma had set up her stand there. People walked around. Birds flapped between buildings, and chirps mixed with the mumblings of people talking. Canteen Ma held up her apples for people to buy. Cnockaert approached Ma. She asked to buy an apple. Then, Cnockaert passed the old woman a message with her payment. She thanked Canteen Ma. Ma would get the message to the next agent.

## USING MORSE CODE

Spies used secret codes during World War I to hide their messages. But communication did not always include written words. Many Allied forces used Morse code. Morse code is a series of dots and dashes. The dots and dashes can be made using sound or light. The code forms letters. Train captains sometimes used this code during the war. They opened and closed their **fireboxes** to tell Allied soldiers where German forces were located.

# CHAPTER FOUR

# EDITH CAVELL

E dith Cavell's feet were sore. It had been a long day at the Belgian hospital where she worked, and it was not over yet. It was 1914, and even though the war was still new, it felt like it had been going for years. German soldiers patrolled the streets. New laws were printed on posters and German soldiers hammered them onto walls. The newest one stated that no one was allowed to hide Allied soldiers. Cavell did not agree with the Central powers, but she did not know how to help.

That night, Cavell walked around the hospital and checked on the wounded German soldiers there. Then, three men cautiously entered the hospital. One was suffering from a leg wound and limped toward her. Another had stuffed clothing into a hump on his back. He had done this to avoid questions from German soldiers who might wonder why he was not in the army.

◄ **Edith Cavell was from England.**

▲ Cavell (front row, left) ran a nurse training school in Belgium.

The third man pulled Cavell aside. He explained to her that the two men he was with were British soldiers. They were trapped in Belgium and needed a way out. Allied soldiers could not get out of Belgium because German forces arrested them if they were found. The man asked Cavell to help them.

A statue of Cavell was put up in London, ▶ England, to celebrate her work.

Cavell agreed and hid the two men for weeks. In the meantime, Cavell continued helping Germans at the hospital. She also found a guide willing to bring the soldiers over the border into the Netherlands. The two soldiers were eventually snuck out of the city.

Under Cavell, the hospital become a secret shelter for Allied soldiers. She pretended the men were patients there and gave them fake identification cards before helping them escape to the Netherlands.

Sometimes, Germans unexpectedly came to her hospital to look around. Cavell would have to quickly move Allied soldiers out of the building. One time, Cavell hid a British soldier in a wooden barrel. She dumped apples over him until he was hidden. Her heart pounded quickly as the Germans searched the hospital. If they found out what she was doing, Cavell could be put in prison or killed. But the Germans left without discovering anything.

After hiding them, Cavell would bring the Allied soldiers to guides who would help them escape German-occupied territory. One evening, Cavell took her dog for a walk. She made her way down the street and nodded at the German soldiers she passed. Some Allied soldiers were walking far behind her.

They were dressed on old, ragged clothing. But no one suspected who they were.

They reached the edge of town. The soldiers paused next to Cavell. A man appeared from the forest. He was the guide. Cavell wished the soldiers good luck and safety. They disappeared into the trees. At the time, Cavell had no idea that she would go on to help more than 200 Allied soldiers get to safety.

## THINK ABOUT IT

► Do you think the war would have been different without female spies? Explain your answer.
► Secret codes kept spies and messages safe. What kind of codes do people use today?
► Do you think spies are needed in times of peace? Why or why not?

# GLOSSARY

**acids (AS-ids):** Acids are types of chemicals. Some acids that are mixed together can cause fires.

**ammunition (am-yuh-NISH-uhn):** Bullets for guns are known as ammunition. Von Rintelen used small bombs to set fires in ships carrying ammunition.

**checkpoint (CHEK-point):** A checkpoint is a place where people or vehicles are stopped and searched by an official before they can pass. De Bettignies had to make it past the checkpoint with her secret message.

**evidence (EV-i-duhns):** Information that helps prove if something is true is called evidence. Von Rintelen did not want to leave behind evidence of his activities.

**fireboxes (FIRE-bahk-zes):** Fireboxes are areas in trains where wood or coal is burned to power the train's engine. Train captains opened and closed fireboxes to deliver their messages in Morse code.

**neutral (NOO-truhl):** Neutral means to not support either side in a conflict. Some European countries were neutral in World War I.

**recruit (ri-KROOT):** To recruit means to try to get someone to join something. Von Rintelen wanted to recruit people to his mission.

**telegrams (TEL-i-grams):** Telegrams are messages sent through a telegraph. During the war, some telegrams were sent in code to hide secret information from the opposing side.

# TO LEARN MORE

## BOOKS

Kenney, Karen Latchana. *Everything World War I.*
Washington, DC: National Geographic Society, 2014.

O'Keefe, Emily. *Eyewitness to the Assassination of Archduke Francis Ferdinand.* Mankato, MN: The Child's World, 2018.

Rasmussen, R. Kent. *World War I for Kids: A History with 21 Activities.* Chicago, IL: Chicago Review Press, 2014.

## WEBSITES

Visit our website for links about World War I: childsworld.com/links

*Note to Parents, Teachers, and Librarians: We routinely verify our Web links to make sure they are safe and active sites. So encourage your readers to check them out!*

## SELECTED BIBLIOGRAPHY

King, Melanie. "Thanks for the Spycraft, World War I." *Boston Globe*, 3 Aug. 2014, bostonglobe.com. Accessed 18 Sept. 2019.

Rintelen, Franz von. *The Dark Invader: Wartime Reminiscences of a German Naval Intelligence Officer.* Dickson Limited, 1933.

"World War I Fast Facts." *CNN*, 30 July 2019, cnn.com. Accessed 18 Sept. 2019.

# INDEX

## ABOUT THE AUTHOR

Martha London lives in Minnesota. Martha is a writer and educator. She has written more than 100 books for young readers. When she isn't writing or teaching, you can find her hiking in the woods.